Imitating *Nature*

From Penguin Wings to
Boat Flippers

Other books in this series include:

From Barbs on a Weed to Velcro
From Bat Sonar to Canes for the Blind
From Bug Legs to Walking Robots
From Spider Webs to Man-Made Silk

Imitating *Nature*

From Penguin Wings to Boat Flippers

Toney Allman

KIDHAVEN PRESS

An imprint of Thomson Gale, a part of The Thomson Corporation

THOMSON

™

GALE

Detroit • New York • San Francisco • San Diego • New Haven, Conn. • Waterville, Maine • London • Munich

For more information, contact
KidHaven Press
27500 Drake Rd.
Farmington Hills, MI 48331-3535
Or you can visit our Internet site at http://www.gale.com

LIBRARY OF CONGRESS CATALOGING-IN-PUBLICATION DATA
Allman, Toney.
From penguin wings to boat flippers / by Toney Allman.
p. cm. — (Imitating nature)
Includes bibliographical references and index.
ISBN 0-7377-3386-1 (hardcover : alk. paper)
1. Flipper propulsion (Marine engineering)—Juvenile literature. I. Title. II. Series.
VM562.A44 2006
623.87'3—dc22
2005007383

Printed in The United States of America

Contents

CHAPTER 1

Grace in the Sea

No boat, ship, or submarine can move through water like a penguin can. Penguins speed through their watery homes with an ease that people have long admired. At Massachusetts Institute of Technology (MIT), Michael Triantafyllou wants to design a water vessel that moves like a penguin. He and his team at MIT's Ocean Engineering Laboratory want clumsy, stiff water vessels to imitate graceful, swimming penguins. Studying penguins was the first step to building a better boat.

Penguins Rule

Seventeen different kinds of penguins live in the world. They live in places such as Antarctica, the Galápagos Islands, Australia, and the tip of South America. Most are black with white breasts, and they come in all different sizes. The largest is the emperor penguin, at 48 inches (120cm) tall. The smallest is

With their powerful flippers, these king penguins swim through the water with ease.

the little blue penguin, which is only 16 inches (41 cm) tall.

Penguins are birds, but they do not fly through the air. They walk on land and seem to fly through water. On land, a penguin looks clumsy. It waddles along on its two feet or slides across snow on its belly. In water, however, a penguin moves smoothly and gracefully.

Penguins have stiff wings called flippers. Their flippers flap and push hard against the water. This strong pushing is called **thrust**. Even though the thrust is powerful, it is very smooth. The water pushed backward by a swimming penguin does not swirl back around its flippers and get churned up and bubbly. It flows behind each flipper in a small stream called a **wake**. A rough wake would swirl around each flipper, make it hard to push, and tire out the penguin. With its smooth wake, a penguin does not waste energy fighting whirling water.

Flexible Flippers

Each flipper is attached to the penguin's body by a **joint** that is similar to a person's shoulder.

Penguins have streamlined bodies and stiff wings, making them well-suited to a life in the sea.

From Penguin Wings to Boat Flippers

This kind of joint allows the flippers to bend and twist in different directions. The flippers flap up and down like other birds' wings. They also move forward and backward and twist around to propel, turn, and stop the penguin's body.

A swimming emperor penguin moves easily at about 6.8 miles (11km) per hour. Even the little blue penguin usually swims at speeds of 4 miles (6.5km) per hour. A penguin rushing to escape an enemy is even speedier, achieving speeds of 14 miles (22.5km) an hour. That is four times faster than the strongest human swimmer.

Speed is not the only advantage of flexible flippers. A swimming penguin can rotate one flipper in one direction and the other flipper in another direction. This allows it to turn instantly

Porpoising Along

Penguins can use their flippers to porpoise like a dolphin when they need to come out of the water to take a breath or swim fast to escape an enemy. Porpoising means that a penguin leaps in and out of the water while swimming. To do this, the penguin swims speedily under water and then pushes out of the water with its flippers in a graceful arc that lasts about half a second. Penguins can porpoise over and over as they swim along.

A porpoising emperor penguin shoots out of the water.

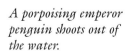

and stop in a second. With a powerful thrust of its flippers, a penguin can hurl itself 6 feet (1.8m) out of the water onto an iceberg. It can dive 900 feet (275m) deep into the ocean and twist its flippers to hover in one spot in rough waters. No boat, ship, or submarine can do the things a penguin can, because these vessels use **propellers**, not flippers, to move through water.

Boat Propellers

Most boats move with propellers that are turned by engines. A propeller looks like a fan. Its blades spin around and thrust against the water to move the vessel forward. The thrust of propellers is strong and moves even the biggest ship powerfully through the water. Propellers push well in a straight line, but propeller-driven boats are slow to make turns or to stop. Also, propellers create a large, rough wake with choppy,

Penguins use their flexible flippers to twist and turn while they dart through the water and feed on fish.

Smooth Swimmer!
How a Penguin Uses Its Flippers to Swim.

Penguins are birds that have stiff wings called flippers. Penguins use their flippers to swim.

When the penguin swims, it flaps its flippers forward and back, as well as up and down. In this way, the animal is able to thrust itself through the water.

The penguin's strong flippers allow the bird to swim fast and smooth, leaving a small wake of moving water in its path.

The penguin is also able to move its two flippers in opposite directions. This enables the bird to turn quickly, or to stop instantly.

Natural Swimmers

Penguin babies, called chicks, are born on land. Their parents care for them until they are fully feathered and strong enough to swim. When the chicks are seven to nine weeks old, they dive into the sea and fly through the water like experts.

bubbling water that is hard for the propellers to push against and wastes energy. Powerful as they are, propellers are just not as good as flippers are for moving through water.

Flippers Instead

No propeller can thrust as smoothly as flippers can. No ship or boat can turn instantly or come to an immediate stop. No submarine can hold still in rough water or leap onto shore. Building water vessels with flippers could capture some of the penguin's remarkable abilities.

Emperor penguins speed underwater, leaving a smooth wake behind them.

CHAPTER 2

Building Flippers

For years, Michael Triantafyllou and his students at MIT studied different swimming creatures such as fish, sea turtles, sea lions, and penguins. To learn their secrets for moving through water, Triantafyllou's team designed **prototypes**, or models, of some of the creatures they studied.

RoboTuna

One of their first projects was a fish-shaped robot they called RoboTuna. It is about 44 inches (112cm) long with aluminum bones, a heavy, stretchy cloth skin, and six motors hooked to steel cables for muscles. This robot fish helped Triantafyllou and his team learn about swimming motion and how a fish tail thrusts through water.

RoboTuna was tested in MIT's Ocean Engineering Towing Tank, a large pool measuring 108 feet

One of Michael Triantafyllou's students experiments with a robot fish. The robotic tail propels the artificial fish forward (inset)

(33m) long, 8.5 feet (2.6m) wide, and 4.5 feet (1.4m) deep. The scientists made waves in the tank so they could watch RoboTuna swim in rough water. Its robotically controlled tail easily thrust through the waves. It moved as well as any propeller-driven boat. Its strong thrust made a smooth wake and did not waste as much energy as propellers do.

How About Penguins?

RoboTuna was a successful imitation fish, but it was not a very good model for building a better boat. Fish and RoboTuna move their tails by wiggling their bodies. Boats and submarines cannot wiggle. Triantafyllou and one of his students, Jim Czarnowski, looked for a better animal to imitate. Czarnowski went to the New England Aquarium in Boston and watched penguins. Penguins

A member of the team that built RoboTuna looks at a display that shows the inner workings of the robot.

These scientists are building a more powerful version of RoboTuna that imitates the thrust of a real tuna's tail.

have stiff, streamlined bodies, just like boats do. Czarnowski made videotapes of penguins swimming and carefully studied them. Then he combined what he had learned from penguins and RoboTuna and tried to build a vessel that used flippers.

Designing a vessel that thrusts with flippers instead of a propeller was not easy. Czarnowski had to figure out the best flipper shape and learn what materials would make the best artificial flippers. The flippers had to be just right—not too floppy, but not too stiff. Next, the flippers had to be attached to the vessel with some kind of joint that would allow the flippers to move in different directions. Finally all the flipper move-

From Penguin Wings to Boat Flippers

ments had to be controlled with motors and wiring. If the engine system were too complicated, it would break down too easily and be impractical.

The Penguin Boat

Finally, in the spring of 1997, Czarnowski's prototype, Proteus the Penguin Boat, was finished. Instead of a propeller, it had two artificial flippers, called **foils**. The boat was 12 feet (3.7m) long and had two stiff foils at its rear. Having two foils at the back was different from penguin flippers attached on each side of the body. Rear foils were easier for Czarnowski to build, and he thought they would work. The foils were run by four motors that were attached to two car batteries for power. Two of the motors moved the foils back and forth, toward and away from each other. The other two motors made the foils twist slightly, as penguin flippers do.

Czarnowski took Proteus to the Charles River in Boston for its first test voyage. He carefully slipped Proteus into the water. The boat was too small and narrow to hold a person, so Czarnowski stayed on a pier and controlled it remotely. Once he started the

Old Man of the Sea

Proteus the Penguin Boat is named after the god Proteus in Greek mythology. Proteus was an old man who lived in the sea. He could change his shape into anything. Proteus the Penguin Boat cannot change shape, but its foils are a big change in shape from propellers.

Proteus the Penguin Boat

Unlike other boats, Proteus uses artificial penguin flippers to move through the water.

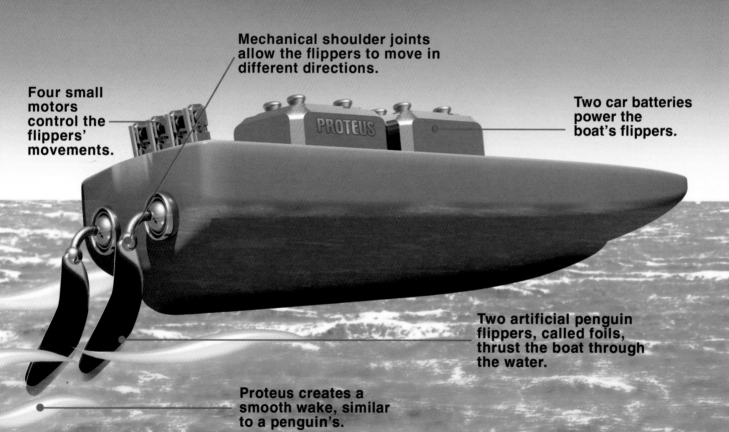

Mechanical shoulder joints allow the flippers to move in different directions.

Four small motors control the flippers' movements.

Two car batteries power the boat's flippers.

PROTEUS

Two artificial penguin flippers, called foils, thrust the boat through the water.

Proteus creates a smooth wake, similar to a penguin's.

motors, Proteus zipped from one pier to another as fast as any propeller-driven boat. Even better, it made a smooth wake and wasted little energy.

Proteus had foils that moved in just two directions, so it could only travel in a straight line. Designing a boat with foils that turned the boat in different directions

Jim Czarnowski guides Proteus by remote control as it makes its first voyage on the Charles River.

would take more motors, a better joint, and more experiments. Proteus taught Czarnowski and Triantafyllou a lot, but they had a lot of work to do before they could make artificial flippers that worked on a real boat.

Saving Energy

Proteus the Penguin Boat was tested in the MIT Ocean Engineering Towing Tank (above) to see how it compared to boats with propellers. Proteus's flippers wasted only about half the energy that propellers do as they push against the water. That is because flippers thrust as strongly as propellers but make a much smoother wake. Boat propellers waste a lot of energy fighting their own rough wakes.

CHAPTER 3

Penguin Power

Between 1998 and 2005, Triantafyllou and his team worked to design better foils to propel water vessels. Other scientists in other laboratories were inspired to imitate penguin power, too. Today, penguin power is a reality not only at MIT Ocean Engineering but also in a kind of lightweight canoe called a kayak. Kayaks are usually propelled with paddles.

The New Kid in the Tank

At MIT's Ocean Engineering Towing Tank, scientists built a robot submarine that combines penguin-flipper power with the shapes and abilities of other sea creatures. It is called a flapping foil underwater vehicle. This vehicle is a big improvement over Proteus the Penguin Boat. It has four foils—two in front and two in back. Each powerful foil is more than 1 foot (0.3m) long. The foils can flap up and down

Stealth

The U.S. military is interested in underwater flapping foil vehicles because they could act as silent underwater spies. Because they make almost no noise or splash, they could pass through enemy waters or locate enemy ships without being detected.

These kayaks use pedal-driven penguin flippers to move through the water.

and back and forth while they twist in the water. They imitate the movement and thrust of penguin flippers.

The body of the underwater vehicle is 6.5 feet (2m) long and imitates a turtle's hard shell. By combining a turtle body and penguin flippers, Triantafyllou has invented a submarine that can do much more than Proteus could. It can turn and twist quickly with its flapping foils. It can hover in the face of large waves or swim in the surf without turning over. Triantafyllou says that the flapping foil underwater vehicle moves as easily as a sea lion.

The flapping foil underwater vehicle has passed all its tests in the towing tank. It is ready for tests in the real world, in a river or the ocean. Someday, robotic submarines

Built for Tight Fits

The underwater flapping foil vehicle is designed to fit into and turn around in small spaces. The vehicle may someday be able to travel around coral reefs, enter an underwater cave, or explore a sunken ship.

Penguin wing-powered vehicles may one day help divers explore sunken ships, such as this one with a huge propeller.

such as the flapping foil underwater vehicle may explore the oceans or be used to clear out explosive underwater mines that threaten ships. They will swim under oceans as easily and smoothly as penguins do, even where it is too rough for regular boats and submarines.

Penguin Kayaks

Penguin submarines are not meant to carry people. They are robots. People can, however, move like penguins in a different kind of boat. A scientist at Hobie Cat Company has invented a kayak that is propelled by penguin-flipper power. Greg Ketterman designed a special kayak that does not need paddles to move through water. The kayak has two flippers attached to its bottom. Instead of being attached to motors, the flippers are attached to pedals inside the kayak. A person pedals with his or her feet, and the flippers under the kayak flap back and forth toward each

Penguin kayaks such as this one speed smoothly through the water with penguin flipper technology.

From Penguin Wings to Boat Flippers

other while slightly twisting. Ketterman's penguin-flipper kayak really moves like a penguin.

People who have tried penguin kayaks say they are very easy to pedal and comfortable to ride in. Moving flippers with the feet takes less energy than rowing with paddles. Because users do not have to paddle, their hands are free to fish, eat a sandwich, or take pictures. The penguin kayaks are very quiet, too. There is no splash from paddling, so wildlife is not frightened away.

Ready, Set, Go!

The penguin-flipper kayaks are also speedy and have a powerful thrust. Ketterman tested the power of his penguin-flippers kayak in a race against two people paddling a regular kayak. One person in a penguin kayak easily beat two people paddling hard in the regular kayak.

Ketterman then had a tug of war with an Olympic champion kayaker. The two faced opposite directions, Ketterman in his penguin kayak and the Olympic kayaker in a regular one. A rope was tied between them. Each tried

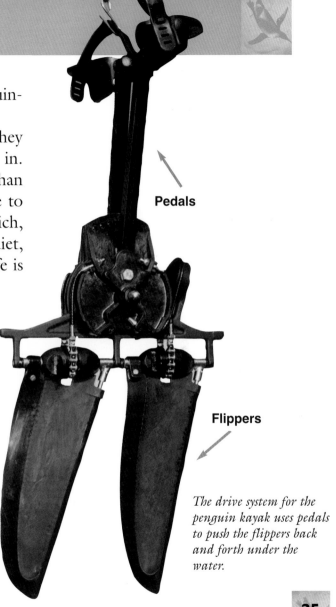

Pedals

Flippers

The drive system for the penguin kayak uses pedals to push the flippers back and forth under the water.

to pull the other across a line between them. The contestants pedaled or paddled as hard as they could. Within seconds, the flipper kayak pulled the champion across the line.

Those Fabulous Flippers

The paddles and propellers that people use today to move in water are no match for penguin

People of all ages can easily propel a penguin kayak without a need for paddles.

Greg Ketterman holds the foils he invented for his penguin kayak. Artificial flippers make penguin power a reality.

power. Whether powered by muscles or motors, flippers create a strong thrust, leave a smooth wake, and turn easily, even in rough waves. People such as Ketterman and Triantafyllou are telling the world to make way for penguin power.

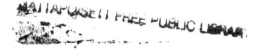

Glossary

foils: Curved artificial flippers that propel boats through the water.

joint: The point where two bones meet and join in a way that makes movement possible.

propellers: Spinning blades that thrust against water or air and propel boats or planes.

prototypes: The first models of inventions.

thrust: The driving force or pushing of a propeller or flipper.

wake: The disturbed water created by a moving boat or animal. Wake can be caused either by the whole body or by a propeller or flipper.

For Further Exploration

Books

Brenda Z. Guiberson, *The Emperor Lays an Egg* New York: Henry Holt, 2001. Two emperor penguin parents raise a chick in the Antarctic snow and ice. This is the time in their life cycle that penguins spend on land. The emperor penguin family is followed until the chick is grown and ready for the sea.

Eric Kentley, *Boat*. New York: Dorling Kindersley, 2000. Follow the history of boats from early rafts to sailing ships to modern ocean liners, kayaks, and super tankers. Read about the invention of paddles, sails, the screw propeller, and other boat propulsion systems.

Neil Mallard, *Submarine* New York: Dorling Kindersley, 2003. Learn all about submarines throughout history and in modern times. Propeller-driven and nuclear submarines are described. With lots of pictures, the author explains how submarines are designed and built and how people navigate under the sea.

Web Sites

Hobie Mirage Drive (www.hobiecat.com/kayaking/mirage drive.html). See videos of penguin kayaks winning their races and tug of war. There is also a short underwater video of the kayak flippers in action.

MIT Towing Tank (http://web.mit.edu/towtank/www/). This is the official MIT site with movies, photos, and animations of the lab's RoboTuna, RoboPike, Proteus, and the flapping foil underwater vehicle.

Penguins Around the World (www.siec.k12.in.us/~west proj/penguins/index.html). This site for kids is full of photos and facts about penguins and their lives. Follow the links in the treasure hunt to learn even more.

Index

Picture Credits

About the Author

Toney Allman holds degrees from Ohio State University and the University of Hawaii. She currently lives on the Chesapeake Bay in Virginia, where she enjoys sunrises, long walks, and learning about the natural world.

DATE DUE

FEB 1 0 2009	
AUG 0 5 2010	
DEC 0 1 2010	
MAR 1 0 2011	
MAR 0 9 2012	
MAR 2 9 2012	
OCT 1 2 2012	
MAY 0 3 2013	
SEP 2 0 2013	
OCT 2 6 2013	
DEC 2 0 2016	

GAYLORD   #3522PI   Printed in USA